MLM SECRETS

THE SECRETS OF SUCCESSFUL
NETWORK MARKETERS

ANNE SCHLOSSER

Contents

Preface

MLM or the Multi-Level Marketing is a conceptual base use in the marketing of the business. It depends on the marketing that has been carried through a network. It explains the meaning of every personnel working in the company will be motivated and encouraged not just to sell the products or services, but it is also explained that these members have to keep expanding their network by employing on more members of marketing to the company and the marketing network.

The concept is beautiful about the business as it is a win-win situation for the companies and the people who have been undertaking the concept. The MLM marketing is a concept that has been giving benefits, not to the people only, but the company as the selling of the products is obtained. The sales that have been made gives commission to the person who made that sale but also the person will get the commission of the sale that has been made by another person recruited by him. The compensation plan is decided by the company so according to it the marketers make money. The new people who are introduced to the worthwhile business opportunity will get the benefits as well.

CHAPTER ONE

What is MLM or Network Marketing?

MLM or the network marketing is sometimes giving people less exciting views. People perceive that this concept is not as exciting as others because it is just used to move the products and the services of the company to other just like a franchise working. People consider the MLM marketing as a mini-franchise of the company where they offer their products and services. In actual concepts, the Network Marketing is a working franchise where the members of it get a smaller level of wage, they learn the business techniques, get the experience and training and then they follow up to start their further mini-franchise. These further franchises are then free to run within the rules, regulations, and guidelines set by the particular company itself. The franchises just have to align their interests and regularize their work line.

The process of marketing and selling the products has been considering some of the conventional as well as the traditional methods and processes. These sales are carried through the direct sales or face to face selling. These both concepts are extremely important when the network selling is taken. In the whole world, the societies and the areas that have people standing in front of each other to buy and sell as it is the only way through which the businesses are done. But in the United States of America, the people who are doing personalized marketing are being sidelined. This personal salesmanship is considered to be old, and it has been replaced by the internet, social media marketing, megastores as well as other impersonal techniques that are used to move the massive quantities of goods and services.

Sorry to say, but there are still some authorities that want slick-talking or unscrupulous types while making the sales representing the historic and conventional methods. The authorities just want the sales to happen. In the 1800s, the infamous 'snake oil salesman' was selling his liquid oil or the type of powder to all the people who have any diseases or even the marital issues. There was no systemized and particular methods of marketing, and that was the time when the network marketing was about to start. The marketing areas were regulating by the help of some regulatory authorizes in the sales industry that helped the salesperson. The sales people were given guidelines about what were they able to say and what they were not about to say. The time was when the direct sales or the personalized sales have a bad name and reputation. They do not have any particular idea how to make sales about their goods and services. The system of the direct selling was due at that time.

Some of the early sellers of the MLM marketing concepts did not have any idea how to make sales. They started with the example of the Snake Oil seller and started selling with the particular case in point. There were other ethical and regularized concepts of marketing in the industry where the expert and educated people were serving their companies by selling their services and goods.

Thos early sellers gave a wrong reputation of the industry that had some adverse effects. These people started their work by overselling, overpromising, outright lying, and overhyping about the particular services and products.

The people were wrongly attracted in the MLM industry. Some of the people were employed in view that they will give a particular amount of money that will help them make money and this also earned disrespect of the concept as everything was based on lies and misrepresentations of the system.

In the early days of the MLM marketing, people had no idea that what they are up to and all the irregular and unscrupulous people in the field made a bad impact. In today's world, still, there are people who made their network by recruiting the people and giving them the dreams that they will get rich quickly. These potential recruits were given a concept of millions of dollars and were told that all the issues of the life would be solved once they well get involved in the MLM industry.

All these issues are acceptable as all the industries do face such issues when they are starting up. They are sections or people who usually exaggerate things that exist in less. They overpromise to the people, and other associates about the things that are not the way they must be. For example, the lawyers have a bad reputation as they make use of the people unethically. They think of people as their prey and use their weaknesses to make their money. They are considered to be the 'ambulance chasers' of that time. But not lawyers are same; some of them are the best example of their industry. They helped people and got to their work like rest of the people.

The majority of the networkers or the MLM marketers are the same. They believe in a particular concept. They think of their products and services that are in daily use and are interested in selling the, working on them and then train their further network of the recruiters as well as employed people. They want to grow their business and achieve the company's ultimate goal. There are still people in the industry who pump the other worker making them believe that the network marketing is the only way that will help them mitigate the problems of life. It is extremely significant that a person must not use a single painting brush to paint the industry.

The people, who are interested in the network marketing, must carry their work just in the right direction. They must work for the right reasons and concerns that help them to build their career and fate. Joining the network marketing think of the success that will be achieved earlier is completely wrong. The desperation for money and other pressures are not the particular ingredients to becoming successful overnight. When a person wants to be successful in his chosen field, he must be working with passion. He must focus on the responsibilities, products, and services that must be sold and represented to the customers. For example, when you are about to sell a particular facial cosmetic product, you must try using it before you go out and sell it to someone. When there will be a practical application of the product, your skin with glow and people would like to see the results that the product has been giving. It will give others the preview of your passion for your work and the relation to your products. The customer will be looking at the products, and they will become interested in the product. It will open the doors to the possible sales, and new employees will be employed.

While viewing the lifestyle, most of the network or MLM marketers will be involved in the sales group completely, and they will feel comfortable and at home with the other members of the group whether they are up or down the line. When the products and the services of the particular company are being used on you, the distributors will become familiar with it. They will start talking about the opportunities and chances that will present them becoming the second nature.

When looking through the eyes of business, it is possible and potentially acceptable to use the MLM marketing or the network marketing to attract the customers and earn millions of dollars. It will help the company to achieve desired goals whether they are in intangible or tangible equivalents. In the real terms and common aspects, the network marketers are asked to earn about modest money and amount. The people who are thinking to get into the MLM industry must have to set their particular goals and targets that are to be achieved but they must be real and factual terms.

Setting the goals and targets of the company is very important, and it is considered to be the basic and important aspect of life as well as the careers. It will be considered later in the book when the MLM marketing and their techniques are discussed.

When a person wants to choose a network marketing company, it is fundamental for that person to look for the company's take on the marketing concepts and perform person due diligence before getting involved in the system. The person must understand the rules and the guideless that the company follows and makes it marketers to follow them as well. There are increased chances that the company you will be working for will fail to achieve a status in the industry. The new companies are usually at risk and stake of failing and not working for a longer period. It is not just a case of the marketing ones, but other industries have such concepts too that the newer companies are not capable of running for a longer time.

You must have no work with a particular company that is still running their business with the kinks of their business ideas. A company who has a working style that can cope up with the problems and issues of the industry is a better one to look. The companies who are already established and have proved that there working track record must be followed for further achievements. The company offers testimonials to the distributors and the marketers who have success. An established and old company which has proved its capacity and ability in the industry will be able to offer more support and better prospects to the marketers when they are starting up their jobs. The MLM and network marketing will be easy to do well when the people do not have to fight for the particular home offices.

It is extremely significant for the marketer to know well about the product and services that the company offers and they have to market them. You must inquire about the product that will it be successful and whether the people will use or not. Is there any scope of the product? Will the market accept the product? Will the product or service have a future prospect? Is the product unique? Is the product a replacement and subtitle of others? If the people look for the particular product in the market, there will be a chance that the product will flourish. The people will look to buy the product or services of the company. The uniqueness of the product and the marketing techniques will be the business to sell and achieve their desired targets.

The companies achieve success through better marketing and advertising techniques. The company usually focuses on their marketing departments as they are the distributors of the products and services and when they are regularized as well as aligned with the targets of the company, much better results will be achieved.

CHAPTER TWO

Pyramid Schemes versus Network Marketing

Network marketing has to be distinguished with other types of marketing. Sometimes the people think they are a part of the MLM or network marketing, but the case is different. People usually get mistaken by the facts that the network marketing and the pyramid schemes are of same types. But these two are quite different. It has been because the people who started the concept of the network marketing did not take it seriously. There was not a basic plan, and the targets have not been achieved. The network marketing was not regularized when they were started so the marketing method developed a bad reputation among the people and they were not able to distinguish it from other techniques. There was not a single pattern that can help the people to undertake the particular technique. This marketing method does not have a particular Performa, and it was not developed like a specific scheme.

These two marketing schemes apparently resemble each other. Some closer views, as well as little digging under the surface, will reveal the legal enterprises and the scams.

These two schemes different each other and there are various points when a person know them; they will be able to resurrect the meaning of the marketing.

It is a must point to ponder that when a business is starting up, the first and initial marketing will lead to sales but these beginning sales will be considered as the warm market that will comprise of the friends, family and the close acquaintances that fall in the close society of circle surrounding a person. It must be significant to ensure that the product or service you are going to sell or market will be legal and legitimate and there will be safeguards for the buyers as well as the sellers and this must be determined before a person's credibility is put in a stake. It must be ensured that the people marketing the particular things will be representing the company that is truthful and legitimate.

There were some specific companies that were able to bring out the facts and definitions that help the marketing and allow particular points in the network marketing. A framework was provided to make sure that the marketing is network and it is advantageous to the people using it.

Here some of the points will be existing that will help to know that whether the marketer representing a company is presenting a legitimate opportunity or not.

Initial Investment

The majority of the companies who are about to work in the particular market will need some initial investment. This start up fees might include the demonstration kits as well as some sales kits. They are adequate in fees and tolerable by the company when they are not excessive. But when the pyramid schemes are incorporated, a huge sum of money will be needed that are sometimes refer to the charges of inventory. In this case, some of the companies are not able to give buy-back or take-back policies. So be careful about those particular companies.

Product

Let's check that whether the product is useful or not? Is the product valued and in demand and will it be sold easily to the buyers? But before you are taking the job of distributing the products of that company, make sure you look for the product. The understanding of the product is very important, and the market must be observed. There must be a proper plan that is devised before a product is launched and the distributors are asked to sell it in a particular market. The market conditions and the target customers are watched out carefully before any further step is taken. It must be looked that whether the company is offering any of the guarantees and customer services after the product is sold. Does the company give refunds? If all these things are negative, and there is no to the questions, then the company is not respecting and honoring its customers. As well as the company is giving a headache to their employees.

Requirement of the Inventory

If the company is requiring the upfront purchase of the goods that is in large quantities, then it must be representing the pyramid schemes. Inventory loading is a concept that makes the distributors buy their products for the commission and then selling it to oneself.

Training of the Employees

Is the company offering any training and workshops to its distributors? Or any of the workshops have been arranged for the novices, veterans, and the intermediary sellers? Do the companies provide the materials needed for the training and development> or if you have to purchase them, are they overpriced or reasonable?

Deliberation

Is the company deliberated towards the recruiting or selling? The companies that recruit more people are pyramid schemes while the companies that are following the sales is the MLM marketing. Different pyramid schemes are using the goods and services to appear being legal but they are building on the recruitment. If the company is offering commissions for the recruitment or paying not for sales but the recruits, they are likely to be dealing in the pyramid.

Sales

What makes a sale? Retail sales are the ones that sell the products to the people not to oneself. Does the company want the distributors to get involved in the company, their decisions, and the management? If these companies are looking for the active participation of the marketers in their business, so the targets and goals will be aligned, then it seems legal.

Earnings Representation compared to Expectation

The company who is creating hype about the incomes and claiming the distributors about the potential income will be shady. There are proper documents and legal statistics that help the distributors to verify that there is a proper track record of the marketing. The earnings of the distributors and their trends will be visible. The representation and expectation of the earnings will be same according to the historical bases presented by the company. There must be modest earnings that are likely to get, and this seems to be legally true and factual.

CHAPTER THREE

Marketing Skills and Development

Ordinary people can sometimes do extraordinary things which a great set of skills can do. The people who incorporate the skills and develop themselves into a modified marketer can create wonderful benchmarks. These are the people who can use their skill resources to make their work more interesting and get most out of it. These particular skills are required to do something in life. They have been looking forward to training themselves so that their job will not suffer and the can achieve their personal goals aligned with the company goals. The particular skills and expertise that are needed to maximum the outcome and achieve the results that a business wants to achieve are discussed.

Influence

Some of the experts in the marketing business claim that the leadership is an actual influence. It could be more, or it could be less, but it is influencing. Everything depends on leadership and it could rise and fall because of it. It is an attribute that has to lead the world to get the success. Leadership is very important as it could be the skill that can be used effectively to sell the products. It can persuade and communicate to the people successfully about the goods and services that the person is selling. It will help achieve the customers to say yes to the product. And the Yes to any product or service is very important.

Skills

There are some specific set of skills that are important to be a marketer. These technical skills will help the marketer to have his influence on the job. They are needed irrespective of the industry you are working. These special skills will help the person to learn about the outsourcing the thing that makes the sense towards the outsourcing. It is like you can perform on the business while working in the business. These skills are just a smaller part that is needed to get the success and achieve the targets.

Focus

In the fast pace society, when the things are rapidly changing, the skill of focusing the things is becoming rare because the people are all over the places. There are different forces that let them get easily distracted. Time management is not an important skill. All the people can focus on the time when it is already managed in the 24-hour day. The focus management is the challenge that has to take by a person, and it has to be managing well. A person must look forward to staying focused, and there must be topic or agenda that must be concentrated. You need to get a mentor that will assist you in this skill.

Work Ethic

The work ethics is very important as you need to build up the tolerance levels to work in a particular field. If you love your work, your work will become you playing a part. The success comes before the work is only possible in the dictionary. So a person needs to follow the work ethics.

Belief

You are a creator when you are a business person. The entrepreneur needs to have particular skills that will turn the intangible ideas into the physical and tangible equivalents. You just need to take your belief forward. The universe is about to make you believe that you can get the things you want when you are focused on your work and have particular kind of belief.

Faith

The faith is very important to when you will have faith or belief in something; you brain will be able to translate the desires that are intangible in the tangible or physical equivalents. These might be in the form of the success and money or other counterparts. The entrepreneurship and the marketer need to have faith in the particular things and their targets that they want to achieve.

Communication

The people who have better communication skills can do wonders. They know how to convey their messages to the customers who are willing and unwilling to buy your products and services. The communications have the ability to convert the no of the customers in yes.

These particular skills, when achieved, can help you get your desired achievements. The marketing skills are very important.

CHAPTER FOUR

The 7 Step Plan

The Multi-Level Marketing is a business framework that has been used by the company that employs the marketers and the distributors to sell the products and services of the company to the customers. These marketers then recruit other people to add to the network and follow up more market. Some of the biggest companies across the globe have been undertaking the particular marketing method to achieve their company sales targets. The personal targets and aims will reveal that whether the business will find real success or not.

The 7-step plan is the one that will help the marketer to achieve success through the MLM marketing, and the companies will take on these techniques more.

1. Know the Meaning of the Business Success

What business success means to you is the main point that will tell whether what the goals is that has to achieve. What the business want to achieve will tell how the marketing plans will be made. The decisions about the distribution, marketing and advertisement are dependent on the thinking of the business person and the marketer that wants to achieve something. If the business has no tough goals, then the further recruited people will not take it seriously as well. It will create issues.

2.   Creation of Schedule that will help for MLM Success

The commitment is very important. The person who wants to achieve some levels of success and money will create a schedule that will help define the income levels that needs to be achieved and the commitment that needs to follow.

3.   Advantages of the Training must be taken

The MLM marketing undertaken by some companies design particular workshops and training ideas to help the marketers and the distributors to achieve the success. The company usually looks for the training that has to be given to the people particularly in the sales and product knowledge. The distributors must use the brochures, manuals as well as the media that has been provided by the company. The people who want to achieve the sales by doing the marketing must need to take as much information and knowledge from the training as they can.

4.   Utilize the Marketing Tools

The people who want to be successful in the getting the target sales level must use the marketing tools provided by the company. Remember, these tools are provided because they have a fact-based design behind it. They are provided so that the maximum outcome can be achieved. The people have to use the tools like the company-approved websites, the banners as well as the email addresses. These help to the people to look for the customer bases and the target market defined by the higher officials in the marketing department.

5. Attend Social Gatherings and Events to Become a Better Distributor

When you want the company to be successful for whom you are working, you must share your business ideas and the product information with the people you meet. You have to attend the social gatherings and the events to let the people know about the products and the services your company is offering. You must communicate well to the users of that information as the communication can change the minds of the people. And they can follow the company, and you can achieve the selling of the products and services.

6. Showcasing the Products to the People

The marketers and distributors of the products must showcase them while holding the events. These products can be showcased to the people in the parties and the business events. These products can be publicized in the homes or other distributors' homes. Their showcasing is very important, and it could be lead to achieve the targets of the company.

7. Use the Media to promote the business

The marketers of the particular products of the company make use of the media to help achieve the targets. These medias can be online and offline platforms that can be used to sell the products. You can get the particular information and knowledge from these media platforms that can help the MLM marketing. It can increase the network of the marketers and add more recruits to it.

CHAPTER FIVE

Secrets of Success

The secrets of success are very important. There are some of the points that need to be focused well on achieving the targets of the company. These points are called the secrets. These could be the work ethics, skills or training. They could be specific or general, but they help the most to become a good marketer. It helps the development of the marketing network and marketing techniques.

1. **Be Coachable**

The people who are already successful share the secrets of the success of others. So always try to get as much knowledge from the famous and successful people and make use of it. If the people like you become successful, then try coaching others as it will give more exposure to the marketer and people. The network marketing can become helpful when the things are learned.

2. **Develop your goals, dreams, and objectives**

The people who want to be successful must develop their goals, dreams, and objectives that they want to achieve. These decisions and defined plans will help the person to translate the desires into the success and monetary equivalents. Focusing on the objectives will help the person to achieve the better in life. But the goals of a marketer must be aligned with the company's' targets.

3. Work

There is no achievement with the induction of the efforts and the hard work of a person. The marketer needs to put all the efforts into the job and the task that are assigned to him. The people who are successful work every day, with defined goals and a defined timetable. The road to success has particular secrets, and they must be stored in the mind.

4. Be constantly persistent

Persistence is a very important principle that helps a person to follow the dreams continuously. The persistence is significant when you have to believe that you will follow your dreams. A person has to keep following his dreams, and he has to have faith in it. But when you lack somewhere, you have to be persistent with your ideas and bridge the gaps that are needed.

5. Be social

The people who have more connection will likely to be more successful. When the social circle is increased, there are more possibilities and chances to sell the products. The people who want to sell more must look for more public connections so they can convey their messages and communicate the information about the products.

CHAPTER SIX

Conclusion

The businesses who want to achieve the target sales undertake the Multi-Level Marketing method. This technique has been used by most of the companies that want to have increased marketing about the products and the services. The company wants to achieve the target sales, and then they have a bigger network of the marketing people and the distributors. There are different skills that are needed by the marketers, distributors and the company itself through which they can help achieve the defined targets in the sales.

The marketing of the particular company demands different sets of skills and resources. These can be provided by the company, or the people have to consume it on their own. The training workshops are the ones that assist the people in getting the particular set of expertise and knowledge. The people can enjoy the services and products of the company if they are attracted by a successful marketing campaign. The people who can utilize the marketing tools can market their products around the world more successfully. There are some secrets to success that help the network marketing to become more successful with time. These secrets are essential when applied to the particular tasks assigned to the marketing company.

Disclaimer

Introduction

By using this book, you accept this disclaimer in full.

No advice

The book contains information. The information is not advice, and should not be treated as such.

If you think you may be suffering from any medical condition you should seek immediate medical attention. You should never delay seeking medical advice, disregard medical advice, or discontinue medical treatment because of information in the book.

No representations or warranties

To the maximum extent permitted by applicable law and subject to section below, we exclude all representations, warranties, undertakings and guarantees relating to the book.

Without prejudice to the generality of the foregoing paragraph, we do not represent, warrant, undertake or guarantee:

- that the information in the book is correct, accurate, complete or non-misleading;

- that the use of the guidance in the book will lead to any particular outcome or result.

Limitations and exclusions of liability

The limitations and exclusions of liability set out in this section and elsewhere in this disclaimer: are subject to section 6 below; and govern all liabilities arising under the disclaimer or in relation to the book, including liabilities arising in contract, in tort (including negligence) and for breach of statutory duty.

We will not be liable to you in respect of any losses arising out of any event or events beyond our reasonable control.

We will not be liable to you in respect of any business losses, including without limitation loss of or damage to profits, income, revenue, use, production, anticipated savings, business, contracts, commercial opportunities or goodwill.

We will not be liable to you in respect of any loss or corruption of any data, database or software.

We will not be liable to you in respect of any special, indirect or consequential loss or damage.

Exceptions

Nothing in this disclaimer shall: limit or exclude our liability for death or personal injury resulting from negligence; limit or exclude our liability for fraud or fraudulent misrepresentation; limit any of our liabilities in any way that is not permitted under applicable law; or exclude any of our liabilities that may not be excluded under applicable law.

Severability

If a section of this disclaimer is determined by any court or other competent authority to be unlawful and/ or unenforceable, the other sections of this disclaimer continue in effect.

If any unlawful and/or unenforceable section would be lawful or enforceable if part of it were deleted, that part will be deemed to be deleted, and the rest of the section will continue in effect.

Law and jurisdiction

DISCLAIMER

This disclaimer will be governed by and construed in accordance with Swiss law, and any disputes relating to this disclaimer will be subject to the exclusive jurisdiction of the courts of Switzerland.